The 90 Day Focus:

Your Action Plan for Success

Chisa D. Pennix-Brown, MBA

Iona.
Keep your eyes on your goals. Your vision takes time & God has His eye on you.
Chisa
Lady Bizness

ISBN 13: 978-0-9969698-0-2
ISBN 10: 0996969802
$19.99

DEDICATION

My husband has seen the journey of Lady Bizness. The growth personally and professionally of myself and our relationship through the 90 Day Focus has been a huge impact on how we relate to each other. Maturity, wisdom, trial and error, communication, and sacrifice have all amounted to this moment in time. The achievement of this book is more than just words on a page.

This guide literally took two years for me to experience. He was a part of every nook and cranny. He has listened to more ideas than you can ever imagine. He has read, re-read, and re-re-read this book. The environment of an entrepreneur with a spouse that is not is truly interesting. His wisdom and belief in me has led to this baby. Our baby, "Lil Focus", is now ready to meet you and help you create your next great accomplishment. He is as much a part of this book and process as I am and I can honestly say that I wanted to make him proud. This book is a cycle of completion paired with the evolution of a mindset.

Love Always,

Chisa

ACKNOWLEDGMENTS

Sharita Benson, my *Business #BFF*. I don't know what I would do without our accountability partnership that is forged in years of friendship, snacks, and a will to succeed!

DarLinda Finch, my mentor and business confidant that believed in me and helped me understand the power of education.

Daesha Dawson, my friend that helped me realize how important God is and man isn't. She always knows that something better is on the horizon.

Kiyon Spencer, my brother who lent his power to help this book come to the light. We are the fruit of our mother's labor.

DeLisa Pennix-Spencer, my mother who has become a better friend than I would have ever thought. Your lessons did not get lost in translation. Genes are an amazing part of character that you cannot deny.

Blondie Pennix, my mom/grandmother who was always there to teach the fundamentals of hard work, perseverance, and doing it your own way. She always put me in a place that made it possible for me to see more and be more.

THANK YOU ALL XOXOXO

CONTENTS

I Create My Life!

Melissa E. Watts

THE BIG MISTAKE

The biggest mistake that anyone can make is wasting their time! Time is the one constant that no one can get more of. The **90 Day Focus** is here to help you realize the power that you have when you look at time as an asset. What do you want to accomplish? Where do you want to go? What type of life do you want? Who do you want to be? These questions need to be answered to help you create a plan that will enable you to use your time most effectively to achieve your goals.

What matters is your mindset and willingness to be open to change, creating habits, and focusing on the activities necessary for success. The **90 Day Focus** is here to help you create an ACTION PLAN based on your needs and capabilities. I need you to understand that you have to **get involved in your own success.** You are the catalyst that creates change. If you want to accomplish your goals, nothing can stop you. Recognize your strengths and see where you need help. Affirm that you will be successful and embrace your need to improve and desire to build something for yourself that you will be proud of.

This book is an opportunity for you to do self-evaluation. You can enhance your situation by respecting the time that you have to create your life. The book contains real stories about those who have used the **90 Day Focus** methodology to make real changes in their lives. It also contains charts that will allow you to input your own information, systems to create goals for different areas of your life, templates, creativity coloring pages, and quotes to make you think and motivate you to stay focused.

VICTIM OR VICTOR

The **90 Day Focus** is a plan of ACTIONABLE steps that will help you make visible changes in your life. Together we can create a pattern of prosperity in your personal, professional, mental, and financial well-being. Becoming the person that you want to be takes time, and that is ok. You are constantly in a state of change no matter what you do. Right now you need to decide what type of person you want to be and how that life will make you feel.

Choices are always there. It's your choices that created the life you currently have. Think about where you are right now and what led you to your current situation. Do you just let things happen to you? Did you have a plan that went awry? The actions that you take and don't take every day are what shape your life. It's your choice to make them count. Are you a victim or a victor?

Victim: [**vik**-tim]
1. a person who suffers from a destructive or injurious action or agency.
2. a person who is deceived or cheated, as by his or her own emotions or ignorance, by the dishonesty of others, or by some impersonal agency.

Victor: [**vik**-ter]
1. a person who has overcome or defeated an adversary; conqueror.
2. a winner in any struggle or contest.

These two definitions illustrate your perspective at this moment. Either you are a victim who has been deceived by the ignorance or you are a victor who has overcome an adversary. It's your choice. If you feel like you are in between, I am sure that you are closer to one definition than the other. I like to think of myself as a victor because I realize that I am the one that makes the choices in my life.

This book will only be as helpful to you as you are to yourself. If you plan on being a victim, you should put this book down now and pick it back up when you are ready to become a victor. If you have a desire to become a victor, you will use this book to help yourself and others.

You **Cause** **Your** Own **Suffering**

Buddhist Priest

SUFFERING SUCCOTASH

Let me tell you my personal story and how I changed my life. I am a native New Yorker, transplanted in the South, with an attitude that was too big for my own good. My husband calls me a New Carolinian because I'm so Mt. Vernon, NY in my perspective, and so North Carolina in my business. What does that mean you ask? Well to me, it means that I don't take B.S. from anyone and my word is my bond. It also means that I value relationships and understand that it does take a village to really accomplish anything great. I have always been accustomed to being right and making sure that everyone knew it. I have always been opinionated, feisty, tenacious, and strong willed. However, lurking inside of me was a nice girl who truly wanted to help others. I have always been the type of person that could see the solution to the problem.

I understand why people don't accomplish what they can in life. The secret is easy. People are not responsible for their own actions. We have to be accountable and recognize that we don't do this "life" thing by ourselves.

One day, as part of a college homework assignment, my husband and I went to the Buddhist Temple to gain perspective on the faith. Upon entering, we were greeted by a Priest who helped change my life in the matter of an hour. My question to him was simple, "What are the steps a person must take in order to become a Buddhist?" His answer was so profound yet so simple, "People cause their own suffering and if they can realize that, they will understand their role in life". This statement was a **WOW** moment for me. I thought about that for about a week and internalized all the problems that I have ever had with others. Sometimes, it was really me that was the problem. It was my viewpoint that needed changing in order for me to fully understand my role in the situation. The word suffering has many meanings, but none of them good.

Suffer [**suhf**-er] verb (used with object)

1. to undergo, be subjected to, or endure (pain, distress, injury, loss, or anything unpleasant)
2. to undergo or experience (any action, process, or condition):
3. to tolerate or allow

The Priest gave an example that was simple. There is a husband, Phil, and a wife, Keisha, living in a home together. Phil always leaves the toilet seat up. Keisha gets upset because she has fallen in one time too many. She continues to get mad and starts to harbor ill will towards Phil because of this one simple act. This energy trickles over into other areas of the relationship causing resentment towards Phil because it seems as though he doesn't care.

Keisha is left to continue suffering, when she could simply put the toilet seat down herself. Instead of getting upset, she can decide that it's not a big deal. Every time that she gets upset, it causes her distress. It's her responsibility to effectively communicate her discontent. It is also her responsibility to adjust her attitude to not allow this to effect her well-being. Keisha is the one with the undue stress because she let something that started out as a miniscule issue turn into something much bigger.

This example made me realize that I am in control of my feelings and my behavior. I don't want to suffer because someone else doesn't see my point of view. I want to make sure that I voice my concerns to others and they can choose to listen or not. Either way, I have **power** over my perspective and attitude. Once you reach this epiphany, you will realize that you have the power to control your emotions and actions.

CONTROL
ALT
DELETE

CONTROL, ALT, DELETE

Control Yourself and your attitude

Alt Alter your Actions and look for solutions

Delete Delete distractions and negativity

This is a cute little saying and it is often more difficult than just saying control, alt, delete. You actually have to put this into practice. The first step is to **focus** on the results you want. We will take steps to see what kind of person you want to become. This book can help you organize your life and control the decisions that lead to prosperity and reduce suffering.

The next step is to identify, articulate, and alter the things that are happening in your life that you want to change. Recognize the enablers that keep you from being as successful as you would like. Part of your suffering and victim-like behavior is self-induced. You may not realize that you are part of the problem, but also the solution. You know what pushes your buttons. When doubt creeps into your mind, what do you do? The victim thinks of all the reasons why "this" won't work. They pile on excuses disguised as reasons and never really stick with one thing long enough to make it prosper. The victor figures out a way to triumph over the situation.

Finally, you have to eliminate distractions and actions that cause you to veer off the path of **focus**. People will always be there to tempt you, but you can reach your goals. I realized a long time ago that I wasn't worried about being liked, but what I do care about is about being respected. With respect comes responsibility. Most people are not comfortable having responsibility, but you are responsible for your actions.

Consider the responsibility of being a goal setter. Goal setters are constantly honing their craft and making sure they accomplish what they set out to do. Not settling for the status quo B.S. from people who say "it's always been done like this". Those people kill dreams and they don't understand the vision of a goal setter. Dream-killers can discourage you and provide you with any excuse you need to leave your dreams behind. If you truly want to be **focused** you must understand this one simple principle:

You have to give up something to get something.

Lady Bizness

Now, it's time for you to list your strengths and weaknesses. You need to visually see what you are good at and what you need help with. These skills, connections, and mindsets will allow you to see what you can internally control. Your objective is to improve on your weaknesses so that you can reduce or eliminate them. I understand that you have created some bad habits that you may not be aware of. The tool that will help you most in this journey is being realistic about what you really want to change. You control all your strengths and weaknesses.

STRENGTHS	WEAKNESSES
1. open Minded	1. procrastination
2. Respectful	2. an organized
3.	3. not Staying on task
4.	4.
5.	5.
6.	6.
7.	7.
8.	8.
9.	9.
10.	10.

The way to become the better version of yourself is to recognize your weaknesses and threats to success while **focusing** on the opportunities you have to make real changes. Your opportunities and threats are external factors that you can't control. The most important thing is to realize what may threaten your success and reduce your contact with those activities, people, and places. These items are usually your triggers that will lead you back to the same behavior and cause you to be less productive.

Your opportunities allow you to set your schedule and decide on where you need to be located to get the connections needed for your progress. This is usually when people have to step outside of their comfort zone to reach out to new experiences. Depending on your goals, this will be the most exciting part of this process.

OPPORTUNITIES	THREATS
1. Cone health @ Wesly Long	1. Spending unproductive time on my ph.
2. American C Society	2. Not taking action
3.	3.
4. Every 2nd monday w/ Chissa	4.
5.	5.
6.	6.
7.	7.
8.	8.
9.	9.
10.	10.

Cone Health cancer center @ Wesley Long.

You must look **within** for **value**, but must look **beyond** for **perspective.**

Denis Waitley

PERSPECTIVE

Now we can begin the work that is needed to help you create the structure you want to make your goals easier to obtain. What is your perspective with regard to creating a successful life and bringing about situations that are favorable? Perspective is having the proper or accurate point of view or the ability to see it objectively.

To help you improve the perspective on your own life, I have created the **#90DayFocus** Perspective Canvas. It is devised to help you decide on what takes priority over the next 90 days. Each category is listed to help you make targeted decisions. I can promise you that it gets easier every time you achieve a goal. A sample is listed below and my original #90DayFocus Perspective Canvas is on the next page to provide guidance.

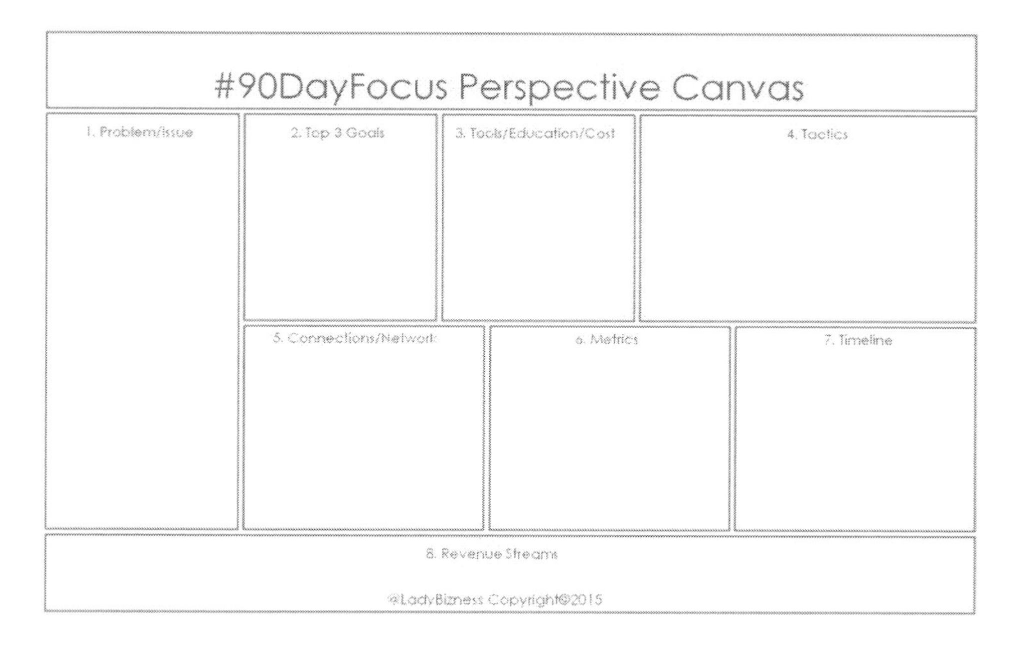

#90DayFocus Perspective Canvas

1. Problem/Issue

I need consistent Money

At least $2000 per month

2. Top 3 Goals

Get 3 Contracts

Expand Branding Efforts

Increase Reach in NC

3. Tools/Education/Cost

Get a New Computer

Better Phone

Update Website

4. Tactics

Update Resume
Take headshots
Update LinkedIn Profile
Slideshare.net
Create Curriculum
Find more speaking opportunities
Sell more Power Marketing sessions

5. Connections/Network

Local colleges
Member Organizations
Review LinkedIn Connections
Seek Business Events

6. Metrics

Get 3 Contracts in NC

Schedule & complete at least 3 Power Marketing Sessions each month

7. Timeline

Start: Oct 13, 2014
End: Jan 13, 2015
Get 3 Contracts

Expand Branding Efforts

Increase Reach in NC

8. Revenue Streams

Contact 1, 2, 3
Individual Clients

Online Courses
Private Clients

Conference
Special Events

Product Line
Hosting Event

PROBLEM/ISSUE

The first category starts off with the fact that there are problems or issues that need to be handled. This section will help you see what has been keeping you from achieving success with your goals. I am certain that there are a number of problems or issues that you want to conquer this year.

This page is meant to help you break them down and decide what you need to tackle in each of the four sets of 90 days in the year. Some issues may not be resolved in the course of one year, but acknowledging them and making an effort to resolution will be helpful. Now, it's time to make your list.

Wanting a partner as if I can't discipline myself to accomplish the task.

Need more clients or higher paying clients

Not enough inventory

Now that you have discovered your problems/issues, please choose the top three that you want to tackle in your personal and professional life for the next 90 days.

TOP 3 PERSONAL GOALS

____

____

____

TOP 3 PROFESSIONAL GOALS

____

____

____

The **90 Day Focus** is a continual learning environment. Keeping our minds sharp and being lifelong learners allows for growth and development both personally and professionally.

TOOLS/EDUCATION/COST

____

____

____

The next chart is an online resource list that will provide you the opportunity to always have free or reduced-cost education that can be used to your benefit.

Online Courses	Description
Coursera.org	College courses (certifications available*)
Udacity.com	Career and technology based learning
Edx.org	High School and University courses
Ureddit.com	Practical how to courses
SkillShare.com	Video based training on varied subjects
TED.com	World views, topics, and education
AcademincEarth.org	College course and video series
KhanAcademy.org	Personalized training for children and adults
Udemy.com	Free and paid* courses in varied subjects
Lynda.com	Paid* service with hands-on teaching
DuoLingo.com	Learn another language for free

Preview each of the sites to see what is being offered that will suit your goals and help you to brush up on old skills. Some sites are self-paced and others have specified schedules. * Symbolizes paid course options

TIP To reach your education goals, you can take one class at a time until you get the desired outcome. The classes listed above are all online, but you should check in your local region for Community Colleges and additional programs that may help enhance your growth. You can also take a class because it's fun and helps you meet new people.

TACTICS

Our next step in the Perspective Canvas is to list your tactics. A tactic is an action or strategy carefully planned to achieve a specific end. This is the area where you list the individual things that you need to do to get to your goal. (If you need ideas look back at my Perspective Canvas.)

WANTS vs. NEEDS

The **90 Day Focus** formula to make sure that you have what you want and need is simpler than what you might think. First you have to look at your budget and see where you can trim costs. Next, visit your salary and see what you make on a monthly, bi-weekly, or weekly basis depending on when you get paid.

Once you have that number, evaluate your list and determine the level of importance for each item. If you are looking at what you can afford, you can see what urgency you need to assign based on available funds. Find out the total cost of the item and divide it by 12, 9, 6, and 3 to see what you need to have in each time frame in order to make the purchase. **FOR EXAMPLE:** I want to purchase a new computer. The computer is $1500. Let's divide to see what we need in each 90 day segment.

EXAMPLE 12 = $125 per month 9 = $167 per month 6= $250 per month 3= $500 per month	Once you review your monthly goals you can realistically see what you can afford based on your pay schedule. Take the numbers and divide them by how many times you get paid per month and you will know what you need to take out of each paycheck to afford your **WANT ITEM.**

NEED SUPPLY LIST

Use this list to define the things that you need over the next 90 days. These items are necessary for you to achieve your goals. For example, you may want to start a business and need a website or you may want to begin meal prepping and need storage containers. Decide on the things that you absolutely need and begin to purchase them over the first 15-30 days of your **#90DayFocus**.

Once you have the items, begin to use them and you will see a return on investment. Total your supply list and make a budget for your needs to be taken out monthly.

I NEED	PRICE/COST
	$
	$
	$
	$
	$
	$
	$

TIP: Do comparison pricing online on sites like Amazon.com and Ebay.com to see if you can find items cheaper. Also, check HSN.com and QVC.com to see if you can use easy pay to get the items, so you won't have to invest funds up front. This will free up some expendable income. Another option for business needs is Fiverr.com.

WANT SUPPLY LIST

The WANT Supply List should probably far exceed the total of the NEED Supply List. This is where I want you to go wild. This is where you put that vacation, that tool, that personal gift, that house or that car, whatever you want but don't need. Once you know what you want, you can start making preparations to get it.

I am a big believer in rewarding yourself especially if you work hard. What things do you want that may not be in reach in 90 days? These items are there for you to have a goal that you can start saving toward. To get the things on the WANT LIST, use my formula.

I WANT	PRICE/COST
	$
	$
	$
	$
	$
	$
	$

TIP: Price does not matter with this list. There may be things that you want personally that do not have a price, but instead have an intrinsic value. It is fine to put those things on this list as well.

CONNECTIONS

I am sure that you have heard the phrase, "Your net worth depends on your network". While that is true, most people neglect to use their network to its fullest potential. In order to align your goals with your tactics, you need to see what affiliations you need to make. Who do you need to contact? Who knows the person/people that can help you? These questions lead you to do some research by writing a list and making sure you have accurate contact information. Once you have completed this list, it's time to make the connections via phone, email, or handwritten note.

NAME/COMPANY	PHONE	EMAIL	DATE	RESULTS

SAY IT WITH YA CHEST

I created a Periscope entitled "*Say it wit ya chest!*" This was my attempt to help others get what they want through communicating a clear message. It is your job to tell people what you need and make sure that they have all the information needed to make an informed decision. Therefore, you must know the details like the 5W's. The "who, what, where, when, and why?" Here is a sample that will help you get your message across to people.

My name is ______________________________
From ______________________________.
I am interested in ______________________________.
I would like to discuss ______________________________.
I can provide ______________________________.
I can be reached at ______________________________.

Notice that there is a section that lists what you can provide. Your job is to provide value to others. Therefore, tell them what's in it for them so that you can entice them. Others items that you want to include, depending on the nature of your message are as follows:

Name of Event	Location	Date	Time
Sponsorship	Stipend	Fees	Description of Needs
Rates	Website	Duration	Expected Attendance
Goals	Partners	Food	Vendors
Gifts	Directions	Contacts	Social Media

NETWORK

Your network is in your phone, in your head, and many other places depending on your willingness to explore online. I would strongly advise using LinkedIn.com as a resource for networking. LinkedIn is a professional social media outlet that connects people via resumes, previous jobs, schools, and skills. It is free to have a basic account, and for most of us the basic account will be sufficient.

For those that do not have an account, I would highly suggest you create one. The benefit to having an account is being able to broadcast your information. Whether you are seeking employment, looking for potential clients, or wanting to converse in groups, the opportunity is there.

For those that have an existing LinkedIn account, you are a couple of steps ahead of the average person. The importance of LinkedIn can be monumental when you are trying to expand your professional connections, but you have to use the platform. Now, you can download your contacts and review them. Look at your connections, job titles, proximity to your location, and who they are connected to. Find the value in their position relative to your needs and make an effort to contact those that are of interest to you. Once you're on the platform, you can connect with me at **www.LinkedIn.com/in/LadyBiz**.

TIP: Request a download of your data using these steps. Move your cursor over your profile photo at the top right of your homepage and select Privacy & Settings. Click the Account tab near the bottom of the page. Click Request an archive of your data under the Helpful Links.

For personal goals, you may want to use Meetup.com as a resource to expand your network. MeetUp is an online platform that allows people of diverse backgrounds to connect via events. Each group has an organizer and they meet a various times to do activities together. Individuals will have a profile and can join any group on the system.

MeetUp provides two options for connectivity. Option one involves simply being a member of various groups while attending events that are of interest to you. Most groups are free and some have a membership fee. I tend to choose option two which is to be in charge of a group. The difference is that I am able to dictate the events that the group participates in. It does cost to maintain a group, but I have found that the connectivity and building outside of being online is worth the monthly investment. One could also monetize the platform by accepting sponsors and charging membership fees. Either option allows you to meet new people with similar interests. Your network is instantly magnified with your participation.

METRICS

Metrics provide a way for you to measure the success of your efforts. The top metric in the **90 Day Focus** is seeing if you actually completed the tasks to reach the goal you set for yourself. Therefore, that goal is tied to a specified timeframe. You can choose to break your goals into a weekly list, monthly, or just use the 90 Days.

Depending on your goals, you can easily see if you did or did not complete a goal. For example, if your goal was to lose 20 pounds, you either did not meet the weight loss goal, you met the goal and lost exactly 20 pounds, or you exceeded it by losing more weight.

You can also have goals that are tied to how you feel. Do you feel better having a process and system to keep track of your habits? Did you contact the people that can help you build your network? Did you follow-up with them to get your desired result? Every time you achieve a goal, measure your success. What you will begin to see over time is that your goals can be achieved faster, which can cause you to add in even more goals or shift from professional to personal depending on your time allotment. Regardless of how you choose to measure your goals, you need to make sure that there is something to celebrate daily. Oftentimes we overlook the little victories that were necessary to reach the larger goal.

POPULAR METRICS

Increased Income	Y/N	Taking a Vacation	Y/N	Successful Connection	Y/N
Increased Clients		Developing a System		Sleeping Better	
Increased Contracts		Reduced Use of ____________		Purchased a New Item	
Began Working Out		Shopping Less		Saving Money	
Increased Spiritual Time		Started Meal Planning		Went to a Networking Event	

WRITE IN YOUR OWN METRICS

	Y/N		Y/N		Y/N

TIMELINE

Some of the goals you have chosen may need more time than 90 days, but you have to start somewhere. Therefore, using the **90 Day Focus** as a tool to stay **focused** will help you reach the goals you have set for yourself. Later in the book, we have clearly taken care of your timeline issues with a full 12 month calendar and plenty of ideas for events, holidays, and happenings to keep you **focused**.

REVENUE STREAMS

Smart people say that you should have seven income streams. The average person has at least one and possibly two. However, I want you to think about how you can expand what you do now into a viable business that can bring in the extra income.

If you are working your regular job, you already know what you make and how much you bring home. What would you do if today was the day that the company let you go? How long could you survive with no paycheck? The answer may scare you. Most people do not have a savings that is large enough to carry them past a month.

It is inevitable that something will happen that is totally against your **90 Day Focus**. It is your job to shrug it off and keep going despite any setbacks. I never want you to think that just because this book is here as a guide, that there will be no more hard times. What I want you to know is that when you do develop a system and have additional financial reserves, those setbacks take a lot less time to rebound from. It's time to think of other ways that you can make money and invest time in cultivating those ideas.

No.

Is a complete sentence.

Lady Bizness

REALLY THO

Nope. Nada. Negative. Never. Not at all. Nix. Not by any means. Hell to the Naw. All of the aforementioned statements are elongated versions of the formidable word, "NO". This word is your friend. When you are making decisions about changing your mindset and getting in tune with the **90 Day Focus** you have to say no to a lot of things. There are plenty of great opportunities out there, but they are not all for you. If you are uncomfortable with your current circumstances, you need to get familiar with the complete sentence, NO. It does not require an explanation. It only requires that you turn down things that are not within your **90 Day Focus**. This includes spending excessively, unnecessary travel, or adding extracurricular activities that do not benefit the end goal that you want to achieve.

I know it sounds harsh, but when you add extras, they take away your **focus** and deter you from reaching your desired goal as quickly. Let me tell you a story about Shana.

Shana is the type of woman that has purpose. She is a single mother of two children, a son in high school and a daughter in college. Shana's daughter was a bit of a wild child. She was always getting into trouble for trivial things. No matter what Shana did to help her daughter, she always seemed to veer off course. Shana's son was a "goody goody". He is one of those kids that try to be extra good because they can clearly see the stress that is caused by their sibling. Her son was active in sports, but wasn't getting all the attention that he deserved because of the pull towards the sister.

One day Shana decided her career was not as fulfilling as she wanted. Shana reached a ceiling with income and felt stagnant at her job. After months of debating, she finally took the plunge to get her Bachelors degree. She enrolled in school online and began seeing that the rigorous demands of keeping her good grades meant that she had to block out the shenanigans and cries for attention from her daughter. Shana gave her daughter an ultimatum which caused her to move out.

It was that day that Shana had finally said ***NO****, to her daughter and* ***YES*** *to herself. After the encounter, Shana prayed about her situation and found that not allowing others to control her life was the key. Once Shana let go of the situation, she began to see a drastic difference in her son. He flourished with the extra attention. Shana finished her degree 1.5 years later and was able to get a new job making more money than she had ever made before. She bought a new car and took her family on a real vacation.*

"IN THE NEXT 90 DAYS, I NEED TO SAY NO TO"

Once you know the things, people, places, etc., that you need to say no to, you can start to be more productive with your decision making. You have to understand that this is the one life you have to live and if you do not make the decision to change it for the better, the decision to be mediocre is always waiting for you.

Being a better version of yourself is a compliment to where you have come from. It shows you how much you can achieve with **focus** and discernment.

Once the NO LIST is completed, create your list of things you need to say YES to. Your YES LIST should consist of things that make you happy and help you to reach your goals. This list may have some new experiences, finances, people you need to meet, behaviors that you want to exhibit, etc.

"IN THE NEXT 90 DAYS, I NEED TO SAY YES TO"

Success is a

JOURNEY,

not a Destination.

Ben Sweetland

THE JOURNEY

You have goals in place and habits that you want to create. Now, I need to make sure that, in some way, you are reaching all the important areas of your life. There may be things that you leave out because you are focused on one particular goal. I believe that reaching that goal takes support. During the next 90 days make an effort to find a mentor or accountability partner. You can also join our private group on Facebook if you need reassurances and daily motivation. Find the group at **http://bit.ly/90DayFocusGroup**.

Life has many areas and we often overlook their importance. I do not believe in the fallacy of work-life balance. There is never going to be a perfect balance, but you can feel balanced. The **90 Day Focus** is here to open your eyes to the areas that you may be neglecting so that you can give them the attention they deserve. Based on our research, there are eight basic areas of your life that need attention.

The chart below breaks down each **LIFE FOCUS AREA** and provides a description of items and behaviors for each. In the NOW column, rate the current importance of each **LIFE FOCUS AREA**. In the FUTURE column, rate the importance you want the life area to be at in 90 days. Use a rating scale of 1-10 with 1 being the lowest level of concern and 10 being the highest level of concern.

LIFE FOCUS AREA CHART			
AREA	**MEANING**	**NOW**	**FUTURE**
HEALTH	Physical Fitness, Weight loss/gain, Mobility		
SPIRITUAL	Religious Affiliation, Beliefs, Prayer, Meditation, Participation		
FAMILY & FRIENDS	Relationships, Quality of Life, Connectivity		
EDUCATION & PROFESSION	Skills, Promotion, Position, New Learning Opportunities		
EMOTION REGULATION	Reaction to Conditions, Anger, Calmness, Ability to Bounce Back		
LEISURE	More time for Hobbies, Activities, Sleep, Rest, Things you enjoy		
CREATIVITY	Taking on new things, Arts, Ideas for Business, New Connections		
MATERIAL OBJECTS	Upgrades, Money, New items, Tangible		

Now that you have your ratings you can use these as indicators of your current levels of focus. On the next chart input your goals for each area. Make your goals realistic and decide on what you can achieve.

LIFE FOCUS AREA CHART	
AREA	**GOALS IN EACH LIFE AREA**
HEALTH	
SPIRITUAL	
FAMILY & FRIENDS	
EDUCATION & PROFESSION	
EMOTION REGULATION	
LEISURE	
CREATIVITY	
MATERIAL OBJECTS	

Tell People

who you

are & they will

believe you.

Lady Bizness

WHO ARE YOU?

Who are you? That is a question that you will get asked your entire life. When I held the first **90 Day Focus** Conference, this question was the most difficult for people to answer. When I asked the attendees why this was so difficult, they exclaimed that they had taken on the personality of their businesses, their spouses, and their kids. They were truly challenged to create a bio that really let you know who they are. Who are you without your business? Who are you if you are not a parent? Who are you if you are not a significant other?

I know who you are. You are someone that is valuable and the world needs what you have to offer. Do you see that when you look in the mirror? If no one told you before, you are beautiful and people want to know who you are. You are the best person to tell them and you do that through introducing them to you by creating your own bio. This exercise may stretch your boundaries that you have set for yourself, but I promise you are more impressive than you ever thought. In the next couple of pages, we are going to have you create three separate pitches that will let us know why you exist and show us the value that you bring to the world.

We are going to use a technique that I teach in my **PERFECT YOUR PITCH** class to help bring out the verbal representative for you. Now it's your chance to create your own narrative and give them something to talk about.

PERFECT YOUR PITCH

When we talk about a pitch we, are actually telling people who and what we are. We are selling ourselves and our businesses to potential clients, press, suitors, and employers. You have to tell people what's important about you and why they should choose you over someone else. You have to be able to articulate that verbally, but the written word has become even more prevalent due to social media. It doesn't matter if you are looking for your next job or client. People will judge you based off of what you tell them. They will also judge you based off of what others tell them. Your introduction to the world, whether in person or online, is important and vital to your success.

I want you to first develop an **I AM** statement that creates a message about who you are or want to be, without actually telling us what you do. You will begin with an ACTION statement that is not a noun. I call this the "**I AM**" statement. This can be one word or a phrase. For example, I tell people that I am a timesaver. My job is to make people save time by making marketing, branding, social media, and business development easier to understand, which provides more time for them to create their successful businesses. Now it's your turn, what is your I AM Phrase.

1. **I AM** a/an ____

This phrase does not give away the kitchen sink. It is meant to entice others to talk to you and ask additional questions.

POWER WORDS

These POWER WORDS are listed to help you be more assertive and succinct in your messaging. Use them if you are stuck or want to expand your message.

1. Absolutely 2. Accomplish 3. Achieve 4. Benefit 5. Best 6. Clear-cut 7. Compelling 8. Convenient 9. Critical 10. Dependable 11. Easy/Easily 12. Ensure 13. Exciting 14. Free 15. Fun 16. Guarantee/Guaranteed 17. Health/Healthy 18. How-To 19. Improve/Improved 20. Instant/Instantly 21. Love 22. Money 23. More 24. New 25. Now	26. Personalized 27. Power/Powerful 28. Private 29. Proven 30. Quality 31. Quick/Quickly 32. Results 33. Safe/Safely 34. Save 35. Secrets 36. Secure 37. Shocked/Shocking 38. Simple 39. Solution 40. Step-by-Step 41. Strong 42. Top 43. Uncover 44. Unique 45. Unleashed 46. Unlimited 47. Unlock 48. Winning 49. Yes 50. You/Your

2. Add a one sentence statement about what you DO.

I do or I help ____

____

____

____

Our next section is where the hearty value is described. People often provide too much information when explaining their services and value, which can be overwhelming for the listener. When conveying your message, if should be easy to understand what you do.

To create a memorable statement of impact, there should be no more than three main things that you do to attract your target. Choose what you want to be known for and paid for. If you change environments you are more than welcome to adjust this statement. On the following page are three possible starts to your **IMPACT STATEMENT**. Choose the one that is most closely related to the message you want to convey.

3. Give a IMPACT STATEMENT that expresses value

(This statement will tell us why people value your work)

People who use my services find

In my current/previous positions I was able to

My services/clients find

Once you have told them who you are, what you do, and the value you provide; it's time to give them a call to action. Now decide what you want them to do next. Below find a list of **CALLS TO ACTION** that you can use to complete your pitch.

- Call you
- Email you
- Visit Your Website
- Visit Your Location
- Set a Time to Meet
- View Your Profile
- View Your Portfolio
- View Your Resume
- Connect On LinkedIn
- Follow You Online
- Introduce you to someone else
- Subscribe to Your Newsletter/Blog

4. **End with your CALL TO ACTION.**

____

____

____

____

You do not have to put multiple calls to action. One is sufficient, especially if you're verbally providing this pitch. You can provide a business card with your contact information, follow someone online, and/or exchange numbers immediately. If this pitch is written then you can list your social media contacts as well as a phone number and email address.

Combine all of the sections of your pitch and put it together before moving on to the next chapter.

BIO

Now you have a pitch that tells people what you do, but it's not the same as a bio that tells people who you are. I am sure that you have heard a great introduction for a speaker that made you want to find out more about the person. You need to have the same intriguing quality when people introduce you. For this exercise, you can look at the bio in a variety of different ways.

- Introduction to others (speaking engagement)
- Student seeking an internship
- Employee looking for a promotion
- Philanthropist or Program Coordinator
- Unemployed or Underemployed seeking a job
- Retired or approaching retirement and seeking new opportunities
- Eulogy (prepare for the inevitable)

Several options have been prepared to aid you in starting your bio. Choose the one that best fits your situation and the direction that you are most interested in. Each example is designed to highlight your skills and interest up front. You can substitute any area and switch the name around if necessary.

BUSINESS/COMPANY

______________ (name) _________________ is the ___________ (title) __________ of ______________ (company) _________________

PHILANTHROPIC / NONPROFIT

______________ (name) _________________ hails from ________ (city/state)__________ and is a strong supporter/advocate for ____________(cause)________________

MLM COMPANY

______________ (name) _________________ is a/an _______ (ranking) _________ at or in _______ (company) _______ he/she is committed to helping you ____________

STUDENT

______________ (name) _________________ is a/an _______ (ranking) ______________ at ____ (school or company) _____with a major in ________(major)_________

RETIRED/UNEMPLOYED

______________ (name) _________________ is currently seeking opportunities in the ______________ (field) _________________ and has _______ (number________ of years experience in ______________ (list qualifications) _________________

NEW PROGRAM

______________ (name) _________________ is the creator/founder/developer of ________ (program)________ with a passion for _______ (examples of work)_________

BIG BIO

Once you choose a format that you would like to explore, continue by adding in relevant work, credentials, schooling and education, notable achievements, and a closing. You can also insert your City/State or region if that is important to the demographic that you are seeking to work with.

MINI BIO

Now that you have your long bio, you can break it into a shorter version that will fit into social media profiles. Best practice is to limit your bio to 140 characters which will fit into Twitter. When you are reducing the aforementioned bio find what is most important and use those keywords to describe yourself. When you write this out, please consider that 140 character limit includes punctuation, spaces, and special characters. If you do not plan on using social media, you can skip this step. However, it is still a great exercise to help you whittle down your content.

If you are using social media, you will want to use the Mini Bio to post on Twitter, Facebook, Instagram, and Periscope. The longer bio should be used on LinkedIn and your blog.

Waste your **MONEY** & you're only out of Money.

Waste Your **TIME** & You've Lost a Part of **YOUR LIFE!**

Unknown

WHAT'S YOUR NUMBER?

There are 86,400 seconds in every day. We all have the same amount of time, even ***Beyonce***. The difference is in how we allocate our time. I am sure that all my procrastinators are cringing, but it's true. When you find yourself saying that you didn't have time to get it done, you are making an excuse for not properly planning. When you are continuously late you are stressing yourself and your counterparts. You could also jeopardize your level of professionalism because others will think that you don't value their time.

What can you do to maximize those 86,400 seconds? There are plenty of ways to get more out of you on a daily basis. The key is planning and blocking out distractions.

- Plan out your week on Sundays.
- Don't wait for Monday to make the decisions on how your week is going to go. Give yourself time to really think about how you want your week to go and put your plan in action on Sunday.
- De-clutter your home, office, car, and anything else that causes frustration. When you have a clean environment, it helps to reduce stress and keep you on track.
- Get rid of things that you don't need. Choose to donate to charity, give to friends and family, or simply discard things that you do not use.
- Plan your outfits out at night. This will decrease the need to scramble in the morning. Choose fabrics that do not need to be ironed if possible. You can also take clothing to the cleaners and separate work and casual attire.
- Plan out your meals in advance. Cook for the week or at least half the

week to reduce your time cooking on a daily basis.

- Find a place for everything. If you label places and/or designate areas for items, you will notice when they are out of place. This will also help you if you constantly lose items.
- Use your calendar. Put reminder on your physical calendar and sync with the calendar in your phone.
- Set daily alerts on your phone to remind you about the **90 Day Focus**. Choose times during the day that remind you to **focus**.
- Purchase healthy snacks and keep them in your car, purse, bag, etc. This will help if you are busy and forget to eat. Our diet is a big part of how we feel and missing meals can be detrimental to your energy levels.
- Adjust your sleep. Go to bed earlier/later and/or Get up earlier/later depending on your personal needs and schedule.

Remember that every good thing in your life happened because something changed. You are responsible for your success and your habits. Time allocation will help you to be more productive and **focused**.

Create your own list of activities that you can do to increase productivity in your life.

____

____

____

____

____

____

Stay motivated by slowing down and planning out your agenda. You can use a physical to do list. If you are going to have a daily **TO DO LIST**, please put no more than three items to achieve in every day. There are typically only three really important things that need to be done daily. Decide on those things when you first wake up and get them accomplished. If you decide that you would like to add more to the list, do it only after you have completed the three. You can also use the Eisenhower method **focuses** on increasing decision making effectiveness.

	URGENT	NOT URGENT
IMPORTANT	1. DO IT NOW	2. PLAN IT
NOT IMPORTANT	3. DELEGATE	4. DROP IT

This method was coined for United States President Dwight D. Eisenhower. The Tasks in this chart are handled as follows:

1. Important/Urgent quadrant are done immediately and personally
2. Important/Not Urgent quadrant get an end date and are done personally
3. Unimportant/Urgent quadrant are delegated
4. Unimportant/Not Urgent quadrant are dropped

To increase your potential and maximize your time you must set boundaries. Give yourself set times to accomplish your goals. The boundaries may be from external factors like people. If you are a chatter box or have those that enjoy lengthy conversations that are not beneficial to your goals, you need to reduce your contact with others. Technology can also be an item that needs boundaries. Here are tips to maximize your effectiveness.

- No phone calls. When you are in Focus mode, do not take phone calls. Turn your phone to vibrate, silent, or turn it completely off. This will reduce the urge to check your phone all the time.
- No notifications. You may also want to go into the settings in your phone and turn off notifications from your apps.
- Do not check your email more than three times per day, unless you are expecting something important. Set a schedule for checking email.
- Use a timer to provide yourself with the time limits needed for completing a task. I like to use the timer on my phone, but I also enjoy using online-stopwatch.com, which helps focus your time.
- You may want to use an app to document what you did with your time on a daily basis. I would recommend using Toggl.com. This system has free and paid accounts. For an individual the free account is sufficient.

MILLIONAIRE IN THE MAKING

Most people set goals that are small and easy to attain on a daily basis. Your big goals need the help of the small ones, but many of us want one of the biggest increases that we can get, which is monetary. Are you setting goals that will get you to your optimal income? Once you reduce your distractions and create a system that works to increase productivity you can really focus on the numbers you want to reach.

Have you ever thought about what it takes to be a millionaire? I am sure that at one time or another you have. I am here to tell you that it is obtainable. You would need to make $2740.00 per day for 365 days. This total would be $1,000,100 in the course of one year. Take into consideration that there are no taxes taken out, and in this example nothing is spent. This is a simple way to illustrate how easy it actually is to make a million dollars. The key is finding something that will actually yield those results. Can you create an environment where you can obtain financial freedom? I believe that you can, but you have to be **focused** on your goals.

I WANT YOU TO CREATE A WEALTH MINDSET!

W = Write down what you want

E = Envision your future

A = Affirm your desires

L = Listen to your inner voice

T = Take action & transform your mindset

H = Hold your vision and be consistent

Let's be about the #2740LIFE and make an effort to get more by being diligent with the pursuit of our goals. At the time of this book going to print, I am not a millionaire. Nevertheless, I have millionaire goals and the work ethic to match.

Meet Derrick. He is a barber and he works Tuesday through Saturday. On average, he cuts about 15 heads per day at the rate of $20 per haircut, which equals $300 per day. Now we take the $300 x 5 days per week that he works and we have $1500 per week. Take the $1500 per week x 52 weeks in a year and voila, Derrick is making $78,000 per year.

These numbers do not take into account days when Derrick has even more clients. To increase his income, he can increase the number of days that he is open or the hours on his current days open. Derrick can also sell upgrades to service to increase income. He can create his own product line. He can also sell items that are complimentary to his clientele.

This example shows how anyone can have a modest income and still are well-off in their monetary goals. It also illustrates ways to increase revenue streams and reach the goals that you've set. Derrick may have more goals like opening up his own shop, going on vacation, adding in another business, etc. He will be able to achieve his goals as long as he stays focused.

To a person that has more than Derrick, this may not seem like much. However, Derrick is able to set his own hours and he genuinely loves what he does every day. Can you say that about your current situation? The freedom that awaits you is on the other side of hard work and planning.

A part of being **focused** and prosperous lies in saving money. You will find charts that clearly illustrate what you need to save on a weekly basis to build a safety net for yourself. You can save for a variety of reasons. I suggest using the charts to accomplish your goals.

You should also know your credit score and always work on improving it. You can use **www.AnnualCreditReport.com** to get your report from the three agencies, **TransUnion**, **Equifax**, and **Experian**. This will not give you your score, but it will allow you to dispute any erroneous information and see what you have that is outstanding. Additionally, you can also use **www.CreditKarma.com** which will provide your report and your score. Take note of your score at the end of each 90Day time period. Scores will range from 301-850.

- Excellent Credit: 750+
- Good Credit: 700-749
- Fair Credit: 650-699
- Poor Credit: 600-649
- Bad Credit: below 600

I'm sure you can guess what's next. You're going to get your finances in order by creating a budget.

BUILD A BUDGET

STARTING BALANCE	STARTING DEBT	STARTING INCOME
$ ____________	$ ____________	$ ____________

EXPENSES

HOUSING	BUDGET	SPENT	TRANSPORT	BUDGET	SPENT
RENT/MORT	$	$	CAR PMT.	$	$
TAXES	$	$	CAR INSUR.	$	$
INSURANCE	$	$	GAS	$	$
REPAIRS	$	$	MAINTENANCE	$	$
TOTAL	**$**	**$**	**TOTAL**	**$**	**$**
UTILITIES	BUDGET	SPENT	PERSONAL	BUDGET	SPENT
ELECTRIC	$	$	ENTERTAINMENT	$	$
GAS	$	$	CLOTHING	$	$
SEWER/TRASH	$	$	KIDS SUPPLIES	$	$
INTERNET	$	$	COSMETICS	$	$
PHONE	$	$	OTHER	$	$
TOTAL	**$**	**$**	**TOTAL**	**$**	**$**
FOOD	BUDGET	SPENT	MEDICAL	BUDGET	SPENT
GROCERY	$	$	DOCTOR BILLS	$	$
RESTAURANTS	$	$	MEDICATION	$	$
TOTAL	**$**	**$**	**TOTAL**	**$**	**$**
CHARITY	BUDGET	SPENT	DEBT	BUDGET	SPENT
TITHES	$	$	CC 1	$	$
CHARITY	$	$	CC 2	$	$
TOTAL	**$**	**$**	**TOTAL**	**$**	**$**

SAVINGS PLAN

STARTING BALANCE	ENDING BALANCE
$ ____________	$ ____________

Once you have completed your budget evaluate what is keeping you in debt. You may want to do the following to stay disciplined over the next 90 days.

- Visit **www.Mint.com** and allow the system to access your existing bank account so that you can see your spending habits. Get alerts weekly.
- Take cash out and give yourself a weekly budget. You can allocate funds for each day and only use cash for your personal needs. I currently have a $7 per day budget Monday-Friday and I can spend more on the weekend.
- Use gift cards to allocate additional funds for gas. Give yourself a monthly budget and put it on the gift card.
- Get monthly transit passes if you are in a city with mass transit. This will often be cheaper than paying on a daily basis.
- Open a savings account that is online and have funds automatically taken out of your check each pay period. You might miss is at first, but once you get used to seeing the reduced amount you just might forget that you are saving. I have **Capital One 360 Account** and you can too. Just use my referral link when you sign up **https://r.capitalone360.com/d31aHqVKzk**.
- Enroll in a "Christmas Club" with your bank. A program like this will not allow you spend the funds you deposit until a specified time during the year.
- Use a program like **Bank of America's** "Keep the Change" with your local bank. This program will automatically round up every purchase

you make via your checking account and add that change into your savings account.

- Set alerts on your checking and savings account with your bank. You should be able to set alerts for purchases as well as specified balance amounts. This will help you avoid bouncing checks.
- Make sure that you use your savings account as overdraft protection for your checking account. This will often lead to lower fees if you do bounce a check or overdraft your account.
- If you are looking for a loan, you may want to consider opening an account with a credit union. They are often more friendly with customers that are looking for smaller value personal and car loans.
- If you have more than one credit card, you may want to see which one has a lower interest rate and transfer your balance to that card. This will save you in interest fees and allow you to free up cash on the other card.
- If you are going to get a credit card, I would suggest **Discover**. They have a cash back bonus that you earn for your purchases. You can apply the cash back once you reach your savings goal.
- The next three pages will give you clear direction to help you save more money over the course of one year. Start saving this week!

52 WEEK $AVINGS CHALLENGE
SAVE OVER $1300 IN A YEAR

WEEK	DEPOSIT	BALANCE	DONE		WEEK	DEPOSIT	BALANCE	DONE
1	$1	$1			27	$27	$378	
2	$2	$3			28	$28	$406	
3	$3	$6			29	$29	$435	
4	$4	$10			30	$30	$465	
5	$5	$15			31	$31	$496	
6	$6	$21			32	$32	$528	
7	$7	$28			33	$33	$561	
8	$8	$36			34	$34	$595	
9	$9	$45			35	$35	$630	
10	$10	$55			36	$36	$666	
11	$11	$66			37	$37	$703	
12	$12	$78			38	$38	$741	
13	$13	$91			39	$39	$780	
14	$14	$105			40	$40	$820	
15	$15	$120			41	$41	$861	
16	$16	$136			42	$42	$903	
17	$17	$153			43	$43	$946	
18	$18	$171			44	$44	$990	
19	$19	$190			45	$45	$1035	
20	$20	$210			46	$46	$1081	
21	$21	$231			47	$47	$1128	
22	$22	$253			48	$48	$1176	
23	$23	$276			49	$49	$1225	
24	$24	$300			50	$50	$1275	
25	$25	$325			51	$51	$1326	
26	$26	$351			52	$52	$1378	

FYI: If you miss a week during anytime, make sure you add in the week before and the current week to stay on course. You can start Week One this month and continue for one year.

52 WEEK $AVINGS CHALLENGE
SAVE $5000 IN A YEAR

WEEK	DEPOSIT	BALANCE	CHECK		WEEK	DEPOSIT	BALANCE	CHECK
1	$20	$20			27	$100	$2060	
2	$35	$55			28	$165	$2225	
3	$45	$100			29	$55	$2280	
4	$125	$225			30	$80	$2360	
5	$25	$250			31	$105	$2465	
6	$50	$300			32	$170	$2635	
7	$75	$375			33	$60	$2695	
8	$130	$505			34	$85	$2780	
9	$30	$535			35	$110	$2890	
10	$55	$590			36	$175	$3065	
11	$80	$670			37	$65	$3130	
12	$135	$805			38	$90	$3220	
13	$35	$ 840			39	$115	$3335	
14	$60	$900			40	$180	$3515	
15	$85	$985			41	$70	$3585	
16	$140	$1125			42	$95	$3680	
17	$40	$1165			43	$120	$3800	
18	$65	$1230			44	$190	$3990	
19	$90	$1320			45	$75	$4065	
20	$150	$1470			46	$100	$4165	
21	$45	$1515			47	$125	$4290	
22	$70	$1585			48	$195	$4485	
23	$95	$1680			49	$80	$4565	
24	$155	$1835			50	$105	$4670	
25	$50	$1885			51	$130	$4800	
26	$75	$1960			52	$20	$5000	

This should help you to have a great emergency fund. Having a $5000 savings will typically cover at least two months worth of rent or mortgage for the average person in case something "crazy" happens in your life.

52 WEEK $AVINGS CHALLENGE
YOUR $__________ SAVINGS

WEEK	DEPOSIT	BALANCE	CHECK	WEEK	DEPOSIT	BALANCE	CHECK
1				27			
2				28			
3				29			
4				30			
5				31			
6				32			
7				33			
8				34			
9				35			
10				36			
11				37			
12				38			
13				39			
14				40			
15				41			
16				42			
17				43			
18				44			
19				45			
20				46			
21				47			
22				48			
23				49			
24				50			
25				51			
26				52			

You can also create your own savings plan if neither of the others will work for you. Just make sure that you save something that will really help you each month.

12 MONTH $AVINGS CHALLENGE

JAN	FEB	MAR
$	$	$
APR	MAY	JUN
$	$	$
JULY	AUG	SEP
$	$	$
OCT	NOV	DEC
$	$	$

If you feel more comfortable with a monthly savings challenge, use this to track your savings.

You can also add in additional money during this challenge and grow your savings even faster. To accommodate for our overachievers or those that want to adjust because of pay periods use this blank challenge to track your savings.

Managing your time without setting **priorities** is like shooting randomly & calling whatever you hit a **target**.

Peter Turla

TIME IS AN ASSET

If you haven't guessed it by now, I am a person that truly respects time. That is the cornerstone of all the meaningful things we do in life. People will come up with a myriad of excuses about time and why they do or do not want to be bound to a clock. I want you to know that you have the time to get your goals accomplished, but it is your duty to make it happen every day.

Let me tell you about Mika. She always said she didn't have the time for starting her business. She worked a full time job from 9 am – 5 pm and wanted to get a new car. Her job was never going to pay her past a certain salary and she needed extra money in order to get the car. Mika went and got a part-time job on the weekends, working on average 6 hours per day. This means that Mika works on average 52 hours per week. She found the time to spend an extra 12 hours at the second job…amazing right?

Mika's story is not "amazing". It's the plight of so many people. When we are faced with no other choice, we do what we have to do to survive. NO matter what your circumstances are, life will force you to make time for what you assumed you couldn't. You have the time. Now it's about prioritizing. My hope for you, upon completing this book, is that you do more than survive. I want you to **THRIVE**. I want you to have the money you need and the mindset to accompany it, but that can only happen if you are diligent in completing tasks.

- Create a daily plan the night before.
- Get a free account on **www.RescueTime.com**. This service will run in the background of your computer and phone to analyze how you spend your day. I like it because it will provide a report every 90 days.

Don't get sidetracked by people who are not on track!

In the upcoming pages, you are going to be able to map out an entire year. Don't be scared! Just know that if you take the time now to think about what is important to you, accomplishing your goals will be easier. You can avoid overbooking yourself and make plans for vacations, birthdays, starting your new business, expanding your existing business, and more.

Each month is outlined as a **SNAPSHOT** and is accompanied by monthly happenings. No matter when you pick up this book, these events will still be applicable. If you are in business, you can use this as a guide for marketing. This monthly listing will help you plan campaigns and give you one year's notice. You may also want to include special events that happen in your region and personal life events. Use **SNAPSHOT** technique to reduce conflict and enhance planning. Once you've completed this task, transfer your physical calendar and sync on your phone.

JANUARY SNAPSHOT

FOR YOUR INFORMATION	JANUARY
Clean Your Home & Office	1
	2
Time to get ready for taxes	3
	4
	5
	6
HOLIDAYS & OBSERVANCES	7
	8
New Year's Day	9
	10
MLK Day	11
	12
National Bath Safety Month	13
	14
National Blood Donor Month	15
	16
National Braille Literacy Month	17
	18
National Hobby Month	19
	20
Hot Tea Month	21
	22
National Oatmeal Month	23
	24
National Soup Month	25
	26
	27
	28
	29
	30
	31

JANUARY **YEAR** ________________

Sun	Mon	Tue	Wed	Thu	Fri	Sat

JANUARY NOTES

FEBRUARY SNAPSHOT

FOR YOUR INFORMATION	FEBURARY
Get ready for the Super Bowl	1
	2
	3
	4
HOLIDAYS & OBSERVANCES	5
	6
President's Day	7
	8
American Heart Month	9
	10
An Affair to Remember Month	11
	12
Black History Month	13
	14
Canned Food Month	15
	16
Creative Romance Month	17
	18
Great American Pie Month	19
	20
National Cherry Month	21
	22
Children's Dental Health Month	23
	24
National Grapefruit Month	25
	26
National Weddings Month	27
	28

FEBRUARY **YEAR** ________________

Sun	Mon	Tue	Wed	Thu	Fri	Sat

FEBRUARY NOTES

MARCH SNAPSHOT

FOR YOUR INFORMATION	MARCH
International Women's Day March 8th	1
	2
	3
Get ready for March Madness	4
	5
	6
	7
	8
HOLIDAYS & OBSERVANCES	9
	10
Saint Patrick's Day	11
	12
Irish American Month	13
	14
Music in Our Schools Month	15
	16
National Craft Month	17
	18
National Frozen Food Month	19
	20
National Nutrition Month	21
	22
National Peanut Month	23
	24
National Women's History Month	25
	26
Red Cross Month	27
	28
Social Workers Month	29
	30

MARCH **YEAR** ________________

Sun	Mon	Tue	Wed	Thu	Fri	Sat

MARCH NOTES

APRIL SNAPSHOT

FOR YOUR INFORMATION	**APRIL**
Tax Deadline is April 15th	1
	2
Week 1 National Library Week	3
	4
Week 4 Administrative Assistants	5
	6
Week	7
	8
	9
	10
HOLIDAYS & OBSERVANCES	11
	12
International Guitar Month	13
	14
Keep America Beautiful Month	15
	16
Lawn and Garden Month	17
	18
National Poetry Month	19
	20
National Pecan Month	21
	22
Stress Awareness Month	23
	24
Sexual Assault Awareness	25
	26
	27
	28
	29
	30

APRIL **YEAR** ________________

Sun	Mon	Tue	Wed	Thu	Fri	Sat

APRIL NOTES

MAY SNAPSHOT

FOR YOUR INFORMATION

College & High School Graduations

Week 1 Nurses Week

Mother's Day

Memorial Day

HOLIDAYS & OBSERVANCES

National Day of Prayer, May 1

Cinco De Mayo, May 5

Date Your Mate Month

Foster Care Month

National Barbecue Month

National Bike Month

National Blood Pressure Month

National Hamburger Month

National Photograph Month

National Salad Month

Older Americans Month

MAY	
1	
2	
3	
4	
5	
6	
7	
8	
9	
10	
11	
12	
13	
14	
15	
16	
17	
18	
19	
20	
21	
22	
23	
24	
25	
26	
27	
28	
29	
30	

MAY **YEAR** ________________

Sun	Mon	Tue	Wed	Thu	Fri	Sat

MAY NOTES

JUNE SNAPSHOT

FOR YOUR INFORMATION

Kids get out for the Summer

Lady Bizness Birthday June 2nd

Father's Day

Summer Solstice

HOLIDAYS & OBSERVANCES

Aquarium Month

Candy Month

Dairy Month

Gay Pride Month

National Adopt a Cat Month

Fresh Fruit and Vegetables

Rose Month

Turkey Lovers Month

JUNE
1
2
3
4
5
6
7
8
9
10
11
12
13
14
15
16
17
18
19
20
21
22
23
24
25
26
27
28
29
30

JUNE **YEAR** ________________

Sun	Mon	Tue	Wed	Thu	Fri	Sat

JUNE NOTES

JULY SNAPSHOT

FOR YOUR INFORMATION ☐ Start school shopping **HOLIDAYS & OBSERVANCES** Independence Day National Blueberry Month National Anti-Boredom Month Unlucky Month for weddings National Cell Phone Courtesy National Hot Dog Month National Ice Cream Month	**JULY**
	1
	2
	3
	4
	5
	6
	7
	8
	9
	10
	11
	12
	13
	14
	15
	16
	17
	18
	19
	20
	21
	22
	23
	24
	25
	26
	27
	28
	29
	30
	31

JULY **YEAR** ________________

Sun	Mon	Tue	Wed	Thu	Fri	Sat

JULY NOTES

AUGUST SNAPSHOT

FOR YOUR INFORMATION	AUGUST
Kids go back to school	1
	2
College Starts	3
	4
	5
	6
HOLIDAYS & OBSERVANCES	7
	8
Admit You're Happy Month	9
	10
Family Fun Month	11
	12
National Catfish Month	13
	14
National Eye Exam Month	15
	16
National Golf Month	17
	18
Peach Month	19
	20
Romance Awareness Month	21
	22
Water Quality Month	23
	24
National Picnic Month	25
	26
	27
	28
	29
	30
	31

AUGUST **YEAR** ______________

Sun	Mon	Tue	Wed	Thu	Fri	Sat

AUGUST NOTES

SEPTEMBER SNAPSHOT

FOR YOUR INFORMATION □	SEPTEMBER
Labor Day	1
	2
	3
	4
HOLIDAYS & OBSERVANCES	5
	6
Hispanic Heritage Month	7
	8
Fall Hat Month	9
	10
National Courtesy Month	11
	12
Better Breakfast Month	13
	14
Chicken Month	15
	16
Baby Safety Month	17
	18
Little League Month	19
	20
Honey Month	21
	22
Self Improvement Month	23
	24
Better Breakfast Month	25
	26
	27
	28
	29
	30

SEPTEMBER **YEAR** ________________

Sun	Mon	Tue	Wed	Thu	Fri	Sat

SEPTEMBER NOTES

OCTOBER SNAPSHOT

FOR YOUR INFORMATION	OCTOBER
College Homecoming Season	1
	2
	3
	4
HOLIDAYS & OBSERVANCES	5
	6
Breast Cancer Awareness Month	7
	8
Lupus Awareness Month	9
	10
Clergy Appreciation Month	11
	12
Cookie & Seafood Month	13
	14
Domestic Violence Awareness	15
	16
National Diabetes Month	17
	18
Pizza & Vegetarian Month	19
	20
National Vegetarian Month	21
	22
National Popcorn Popping Month	23
	24
Sarcastic Month	25
	26
Seafood Month	27
	28
	29
	30
	31

OCTOBER **YEAR** ________________

Sun	Mon	Tue	Wed	Thu	Fri	Sat

OCTOBER NOTES

NOVEMBER SNAPSHOT

FOR YOUR INFORMATION ☐	NOVEMBER
Thanksgiving	1
	2
Black Friday	3
	4
Shop Small Saturday	5
	6
Cyber Monday	7
	8
	9
	10
HOLIDAYS & OBSERVANCES	11
	12
Child Safety Protection Month	13
	14
International Drum Month	15
	16
National Adoption Awareness	17
	18
National Epilepsy Month	19
	20
National Novel Writing Month	21
	22
Native American Heritage	23
	24
Peanut Butter Lovers Month	25
	26
Real Jewelry Month	27
	28
National Sleep Comfort Month	29
	30

NOVEMBER **YEAR** ________________

Sun	Mon	Tue	Wed	Thu	Fri	Sat

NOVEMBER NOTES

DECEMBER SNAPSHOT

FOR YOUR INFORMATION

Clean Your Home & Office

Send Holiday Greetings

HOLIDAYS & OBSERVANCES

World Aids Day, Dec 1

Christmas

Hanukah

Kwanzaa

Bingo Month

Write a Friend Month

New Year's Eve, Dec 31

DECEMBER
1
2
3
4
5
6
7
8
9
10
11
12
13
14
15
16
17
18
19
20
21
22
23
24
25
26
27
28
29
30
31

DECEMBER **YEAR** ______________

Sun	Mon	Tue	Wed	Thu	Fri	Sat

DECEMBER NOTES

#NewGrowth comes when you are **no longer interested** in looking back!

NEW GROWTH

You should clap your hands because you have made it this far. Hopefully it didn't take you 90 days to read this book, but if it did, I'm not going to judge. At least you read it. If you have gotten all the way here you have a much better understanding of the person that you want to become and he/she is **AWESOME**. The next three pages are for those of you that need a little more direction. One of the things that I do not like to be called is a Motivational Speaker. I don't like the term because motivation disappears if people do not have an ACTION PLAN. I promised you that this book was going to help you take action.

In the next three pages you will see a clear list of things that you need to do over your **#90DayFocus** to help you achieve your goals. Please know that everything listed is to help you develop a brand that you can be proud of. I have listed these steps in a very particular order because it will help you to develop your awesome persona. If you have already completed any of these steps on your own, you can feel free to skip those and write in today's date and check it off of your list.

DAY	TASK	COMPLETED
1	UNSUBSCRIBE FROM UNNECESSARY EMAIL MARKETING	
2	CREATE A GMAIL.COM EMAIL ACCOUNT	
3	WRITE DOWN IMPORTANT DATES ON YOUR CALENDAR & SYNC WITH GMAIL	
4	CREATE YOUR BIO IF YOU HAVEN'T DONE IT ALREADY	
5	OPEN A SAVINGS ACCOUNT	
6	CREATE OR UPDATE YOUR FACEBOOK.COM BUSINESS PAGE	
7	PLAN FOR YOUR NEXT WEEK	
8	JOIN THE 90 DAY FOCUS GROUP ON FACEBOOK BIT.LY/90DAYFOCUSGROUP	
9	FOLLOW MY PAGE AT WWW.FACEBOOK.COM/THE90DAYFOCUS	
10	CREATE OR UPDATE A TWITTER.COM ACCOUNT	
11	FOLLOW US ON TWITTER.COM/THE90DAYFOCUS	
12	JOIN PERISCOPE.COM	
13	FOLLOW ME AT PERISCOPE.COM/LADYBIZNESS	
14	WATCH ONE OF MY PERISCOPES AT WWW.KATCH.ME/LADYBIZNESS	
15	FIND PEOPLE TO FOLLOW ON PERISCOPE	
16	PLAN YOUR NEXT WEEK	
17	BUY YOURSELF SOME HEALTHY SNACKS	
18	BUY A PACKAGE OF NOTE-CARS	
19	UPDATE YOUR RESUME	
20	TAKE A NEW HEADSHOT	
21	LOOK FOR A MENTOR	
22	PLAN YOUR NEXT WEEK	
23	FIND A NONPROFIT TO DONATE YOUR TIME TO	
24	RESEARCH YOUR BUSINESS IDEAS	
25	UPLOAD YOUR RESUME ONLINE	
26	SEND A HANDWRITTEN CARD TO A BUSINESS CONTACT	
27	PAY IT FORWARD THE NEXT TIME YOU GET A MEAL	
28	PLAN YOUR NEXT WEEK	
29	DECIDE ON HOW MUCH YOU WOULD LIKE TO "REALLY" MAKE PER HOUR	
30	TREAT YOURSELF TO SOMETHING NICE	

DAY	TASK	COMPLETED
31	WRITE YOUR PITCH IF YOU HAVEN'T DONE SO ALREADY	
32	JOIN A GROUP ON MEETUP.COM	
33	CREATE A YOUTUBE.COM ACCOUNT	
34	CREATE A PLAYLIST OF MUSIC THAT INSPIRES YOU	
35	PLAN YOUR NEXT WEEK	
36	CALL A FAMILY MEMBER YOU HAVEN'T SPOKEN WITH IN A WHILE	
37	FOLLOW-UP WITH CONTACTS	
38	TAKE A FRIEND TO LUNCH	
39	WRITE A LIST OF POSITIVE THINGS ABOUT YOURSELF	
40	CREATE OR UPDATE YOUR INSTAGRAM.COM ACCOUNT	
41	FOLLOW US AT INSTAGRAM.COM/THE90DAYFOCUS	
42	PLAN YOUR NEXT WEEK	
43	TAKE A BUNCH OF SELFIES AND POST THE ONES YOU LOVE ONLINE	
44	TRY A NEW RESTAURANT	
45	WATCH A TED-EX.COM SPEECH	
46	EMAIL ALL YOUR CONTACTS AND SHOW OFF YOUR NEW PHOTO & BIO	
47	TAKE A WEBINAR	
48	ATTEND A MEETUP.COM EVENT	
49	PLAN YOUR NEXT WEEK	
50	UPDATE YOUR FACEBOOK ACCOUNT WITH YOUR NEW BIO	
51	CREATE OR UPDATE YOUR LINKEDIN.COM ACCOUNT WITH YOUR BIO	
52	CLEAN YOUR HOME	
53	TAKE EXCESS CLOTHING AND DONATE IT	
54	CREATE A WORKSPACE/PERSONAL ZONE IN YOUR HOME	
55	BRAINSTORM ON POSSIBLE BUSINESS IDEAS	
56	PLAN YOUR NEXT WEEK	
57	CHECK OUT ONE OF THE ONLINE SCHOOLS IN THE PERSPECTIVE CHART.	
58	SIGN UP FOR AN ONLINE CLASS	
59	HAVE A CHEAT DAY	
60	GET A PEDICURE OR MASSAGE	

DAY	TASK	COMPLETED
61	CLEAN OUT YOUR CAR	
62	GO TO THE MOVIES BY YOURSELF	
63	PLAN YOUR NEXT WEEK	
64	CREATE A LIST OF PEOPLE YOU NEED TO CONTACT	
65	EMAIL YOUR CONTACT LIST	
66	MAKE AN APPOINTMENT WITH YOUR MENTOR	
67	WRITE A SHORT STORY	
68	WRITE AN E-BOOK	
69	CREATE A MISSION STATEMENT	
70	PLAN YOUR NEXT WEEK	
71	START A BLOG	
72	SUBMIT YOUR RESUME TO NEW JOBS	
73	BINGE WATCH A TV SERIES	
74	PLAN A VACATION	
75	PAY OFF AT LEAST ONE BILL	
76	VISIT AN OLDER FAMILY MEMBER	
77	PLAN YOUR NEXT WEEK	
78	CALL AN OLD FRIEND FROM HIGH SCHOOL OR COLLEGE	
79	START A BLOG ABOUT A SUBJECT YOU LOVE	
80	GET LIFE INSURANCE	
81	BUY YOURSELF SOMETHING SWEET	
82	ATTEND A SPORTING EVENT	
83	EXERCISE	
84	PAY ON STUDENT LOANS OR ADD TO YOUR SAVINGS ACCOUNT	
85	TELL SOMEONE ELSE YOUR VISION FOR YOUR FUTURE	
86	VOLUNTEER WITH A NONPROFIT ORGANIZATION	
87	PLAN GOALS FOR YOUR NEXT 90 DAYS	
88	WRITE A LIST OF MILESTONES IN YOUR LIFE AND CELEBRATE THEM	
89	START OR EXPAND YOUR BUSINESS	
90	WRITE A REVIEW OF YOUR EXPERIENCE WITH THE #90DAYFOCUS	

DAY	TASK	COMPLETED

I do want to let you know that the **TO DO LISTS** are truly meant to help push you a little further in the direction of starting a business. Your business can be a side-hustle, a part-time gig, or turn into a full-time endeavor. Regardless of the direction that you choose, you have the tools to help you create the life you want.

GOALS & PASSION CHART	
WHAT DO YOU LOVE TO DO?	
YOUR MISSION	
WHAT DOES THE WORLD NEED FROM YOU?	
YOUR VOCATION	
WHAT DO YOU GET PAID TO DO?	
YOUR PROFESSION	
WHAT ARE YOU GREAT AT?	
YOUR PASSION	

Just remember that Focus is a muscle. The more your exercise it, the stronger you become. Find your passion and pursue to daily. You are the solution to your success. The **90 Day Focus** only works if you do. The ACTION PLAN is here and it's your opportunity to make something great of the time you have on this earth. I leave you with my favorite sign off,

LadyBizness xoxoxo

(Photo courtesy of "Life In Fashion & Photography" By S. Benson)

"SHOW UP & SHOW OUT!

& ALWAYS

GIVE IT TO THE PEOPLE!"

ONLINE RESOURCES

- FACEBOOK.COM/THE90DAYFOCUS
- TWITTER.COM/THE90 DAY FOCUS
- INSTAGRAM.COM/THE90DAYFOCUS
- HTTP://THE90DAYFOCUS.TUMBLR.COM
- REQUEST ACCESS TO OUT PRIVATE GROUP AT HTTP://BIT.LY/90DAYFOCUSGROUP

NOW IT'S TIME TO HAVE FUN & COLOR. HANG THESE IN YOUR OFFICE, HOME OR ANY PLACE THAT NEEDS A LITTLE #90DAYFOCUS. TAKE PHOTOS OF YOUR DESIGNS & SHARE WITH US. USE OUR HASHTAG #90DAYFOCUS WHEN YOU POST YOUR PICS ONLINE AND WE WILL FEATURE YOU. MAKE SURE YOU TELL US WHAT GOALS YOU HAVE ACHIEVED.

COLORING PAGES COURTESY OF LIFE IN FASHION AND PHOTOGRAPHY BY S. BENSON

BOOK COVER DESIGN COURTESY OF ALEGNA MEDIA DESIGNS

DAILY AFFIRMATIONS

I AM A MONEY MAGNET.

I ATTRACT POSITIVITY AND GIVE IT TO THE PEOPLE.

I LOVE MYSELF AND I BELIEVE IN MY ABILITIES.

I CAN DO WHAT I SET MY MIND TO.

I CREATE ABUNDANCE.

I AM POWERFUL BEYOND MEASURE.

I DESERVE TO BE HAPPY.

I AM THE STAR IN MY OWN MOVIE.

I CREATE MY LIFE.

I GET BETTER EVERYDAY.

I WILL SHARE MY GIFTS WITH OTHERS.

WWW.THE90DAYFOCUS.COM

WWW.THE90DAYFOCUS.COM

WWW.THE90DAYFOCUS.COM

WWW.THE90DAYFOCUS.COM

WWW.THE90DAYFOCUS.COM

SUCCESS IS a JOURNEY
not a DESTINATION
WWW.THE90DAYFOCUS.COM

WWW.THE90DAYFOCUS.COM

WWW.THE90DAYFOCUS.COM